About this

I've been working on fine tuning n
some time now and I'm still workin
tips and tricks from all over the pl
my own ideas along the way. I've ....,..... ......
wonderful it would be to have all those tidbits of knowledge,
the recipes and suggestions all in one place to dip in and out
of as and when I am ready.

Beware of the cold turkey approach to going eco/100%
plastic free overnight. Whilst enthusiastic and well
intentioned, this type of approach is unsustainable in that it is
all too easy to give up and feel like a failure. Whereas small
and meaningful changes made over time have the chance to
become imbedded before the next change is implemented.
Changes that are made when you are ready are more likely
to slot into your own personal lifestyle easily and therefore be
more likely to stick.
Let's set an intention right now not to be crazy yo-yo "plastic
free dieters". Instead, let's create a new, sustainable and
ethically friendly life for us and our families.

**Let's be helpful and kind and non-judgemental to others
while we are at it.**

We are all individuals. We are trying our best. The very fact
that you are holding this book in your hands and reading it
shows that you care. Sometimes, a pitstop plastic packaged
meal deal lunch is unavoidable. Don't beat yourself up over it
- just make sure you dispose of the wrapping responsibly.

**Don't try to be 100% perfect straight away.
You are on a journey now.**

Use this book to help you make small changes one step at a
time. Choose one area to work on for now, and let changes
happen when you are ready - don't force it, don't try to be
perfect. Just be open to trying new ways of doing things, and
keep the things that work out well for you. Not everything in
this book will be your thing, but many will be.
Are you up for it?

Let's go eco together one step at a time!

Let's start from here.

Wherever "here" is for you right now.

Let's help each other along the way
and
just continue to try to do better

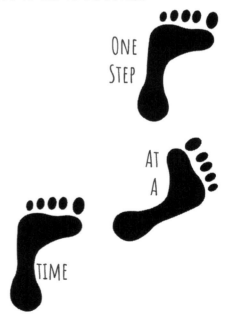

One
Step

At
A

Time

CONTENTS

Mindset shift #1
"Going eco is expensive"

It's easy to assume that all ethical products are going to be pricey. But I have found many ways that have actually saved me money since I started my eco journey.
I've attempted to outline some of them below.

Firstly, **be less of a consumer** and use what you have until there is no use left in it. Get out of the consumer mindset. Try to identify the difference between **need** and **want**.
Challenge yourself to buy less.

Secondly, **Don't buy…. D.I.Y.** One of my biggest savings since I began my own journey was by **making my own cleaning products**. I'll tell you more about this later.

B**uy in bulk** and refill your own smaller containers. This is a money saver as well as reducing the volume of single use packaging going through your house. Bulk buying works well for cleaning products as well as food such as pasta, beans, rice, cooking oil, potatoes, onions etc.

When I say "buy in bulk" - I mean buying larger packets (think sacks) rather than buy one get one free offers which often result in more packaging and are less environmentally sound. This is also a great way of making use of old jam jars, tubs and bottles rather than chucking them out.

Repurpose everything and anything for multiple new uses and refuse to throw ANYTHING in the bin or even for recycling until it is completely past use for you. This will also prevent you needing to buy new products to fulfill those new purposes. An example of this would be making use of clothes which are not good enough to sell or donate to charity into wash cloths, dish cloths, rags etc.

Some examples include; making use of plastic fruit trays and loo rolls as seed trays, jam jars for storing leftovers in the fridge, toothbrushes for cleaning and NEVER buying cleaning cloths again... old clothes are perfect for this job!

Once you start becoming a **bin warrior and jam jar stasher** you will begin to find that you need less new stuff which will start to save you £££. Eventually it will happen without you even thinking about it. You will be keeping a hawk's eye out for new ideas of repurposing waste and fewer items of rubbish will be languishing in your bin long enough to make it to bin day.

Why not keep a diary of areas the in which you have saved money. Each time you repurpose something old to a new use, make a note of what you would have spent on a new product for that purpose. When you make a new product from scratch, what would it have cost you to buy new?

Sometimes - like for like - **some eco products are more expensive.** This is simply because corners have not been cut and ethical choices and quality have been prioritised over costs.

In my opinion, ethical and eco friendly products are so lovely, that to own and use them feels like a treat. I never take them for granted or use them wastefully, and therefore they are valued and enjoyed so much more.

More value = less waste.

Mindset shift #2
"My family won't get on board fully"

Getting your family on board - whatever their ages or your family set up is never going to be as quick or straight forward as you would like. Here's my survival guide...

Don't set your expectations too high too soon.
People adopt new habits only when they are ready.
Think about how long it has taken you to take action on a particular topic.
We all need a bit of time to learn about an issue, understand why it is so important and then to find new ways to adapt and for new habits to stick. If your family don't **yet** understand the "**why**", they are not likely to jump on board with new ideas yet.
Don't worry, it's a matter of time and persistence.
Maybe your son, daughter, colleagues or partner are thinking "What's wrong with how we do things now". It's your job to show them why things need to change, and make the changes as easy and enjoyable as possible.

Forcing new changes upon people can lead to resentment and possible rebellion.

My best advice is to lead by example, and try to explain **why** changes need to happen. Understanding and knowledge must come before intentions and expectations for change.

Educate, educate, educate but be wary of coming on too forcefully - especially with teens (they can be stubborn)!

If you can, **involve family members in problem solving** and shopping choices - explain the issue to them and see what ideas they come up with. E.g. I'd like to find a new toilet paper that is not wrapped in plastic, but I'm finding it tricky to choose which one is best.

If they play a part in decision making, they might just be more likely to jump on board with new changes. You may be surprised by some of the creative solutions they come up with too!

MAKE IT HAPPEN

Talk about the changes you've made, answer questions when they ask. People are generally more likely to listen when they are ready to hear, and asking questions is a good sign.

Let them come round in their own time and don't let it slow down your own progress.
My advice is to continue to buy the things they are used to, but also start to make use of and introduce new products and new ways of doing things around the house.

There are many wonderful eco products which are very similar in look and format to those we are all used to which could serve the purpose of a stepping stone before trying out some of the more radical changes.

Remember your role is as a leader and inspirer here.

Let them smell the gorgeous scents, taste your eco chocolate, see and see how clean the bathroom is etc etc.

Remember.... slowly... slowly....

Mindset shift #3
"I cannot be seen using plastic products ever again!"

A word of caution here…. Just because you now have bamboo/metal straws, doesn't mean that you now need to chuck out your old stash of plastic or paper ones.

Old drinking bottles and plastic lunch boxes are still usable therefore they **must still be used**. Cleaning spray bottle products should be **used up** before you refill them with a new eco alternative.

A plastic straw is still going to end up in landfill and hang around for hundreds of years. Cleaning products will still be toxic to aquatic life whether you have used them or not, so it's best to make use of those you have already bought.

Set yourself the intention of not allowing any old plastic products to leave your home for landfill until they are either falling apart and useless, or they have a new destination or purpose.

Therefore it is even more important that you actually make use of (and reuse?) plastic products as much as humanly possible - don't let their plastic existence on this planet be in vain!

Alternatively donate them to a local organisation in need, such as one for the homeless, or a domestic abuse refuge but whatever you do, don't chuck them in the bin whilst they still have usable life.
You might not "look" great still drinking from a plastic bottle once you've declared yourself eco friendly to the world, but it is important now that you walk the walk … and make genuine and worthy eco choices.

Any plastic product should have the life used up until they are literally falling to pieces before being chucked out.

Use and reuse your plastic with pride!

Mindset shift #4
Greenwashing

What is greenwashing?

You could say it is the eco warrior version of catfishing.

Greenwashing is the term used which relates to giving a false impression or providing misleading information about how a company's products are more environmentally sound.

Greenwashing is when a consumer is misled into believing that the product they are buying is "greener" than it really is. For example using the words "natural", "chemical free" or "green" on product packaging.

This can happen in really sneaky ways - not just in the marketing text for example when a supermarket uses "brown paper" style wrapping - they are sending subliminal messages which can lead to incorrect assumptions being made.

It's always worth looking at the product a little more closely, inspect the ingredients, research the company etc.

As you become more experienced at being "Eco friendly" you will find it easier to spot greenwashing.

It's a process of becoming more aware and better informed. You will find yourself starting to check packaging more carefully - looking at their small print, ingredients and packaging materials with a beady eye. Encourage yourself to question things more and to take a little longer before buying to convince yourself of the eco credentials of a product.

Greenwashing cont'

Something you can do if you are suspicious that something is not quite as it seems is to **email the manufacturer** or shop which sells the product and ask questions.

The more we ask these questions and challenge others, the more aware that organisations will become that they can't pull the wool over everyone's eyes forever.

It may also be that they are a little ignorant of the issues with their product, it may be that they assume that their customers don't care about such issues.

There could be an arrogance that consumers are happy to be misled and happy to prioritise cost over genuinely ethical products.

It is our job to question and open the eyes of organisations as much as it is important to educate our own family and friends. In fact, bigger changes can be made by influencing the big companies - aim high and spread the word when you don't like what you hear / see.

Mindset shift #5
Wishcycling

There is a term I came across recently called "Wishcycling".

I love this term, it captures something I'm sure we've all been guilty of from time to time. I know I have!

Wishcycling means sticking something into the recycling bin that we are not 100% sure is recyclable whilst hoping that it can somehow still be recycled.

Unfortunately wishcycling can cause more problems than we would wish for. A rogue item can contaminate whole batches of materials and ends up adding even more rubbish to landfill.

In order to avoid becoming an inadvertent "Wishcycler" We really do need to get a bit more clued up. Here are some tips on how you can get more clued into your rubbish...

Make yourself familiar with what can and can't be recycled in your home collection.

Did you know that a dirty pizza box with sauce smeared over it is not recyclable. Likewise, the glittery, shimmery wrapping paper isn't either. It is better to put those in the general rubbish bin so that they do not contaminate huge amounts of other perfectly recyclable materials.
Sellotape is not recyclable so try to remove it from wrapping paper before putting it into the bin.
You can find out what you need to know easily by visiting your local council website.

Re-reading your council's advice on recycling is 5 minutes well spent because it is a small, cost free change that you can make simply by being better informed.

Where/How to start?

The last thing I want to result from this little book is anyone feeling overwhelmed and then as a result do nothing at all.

There is an old chinese proverb which says:

"The best time to plant a tree is a hundred years ago.
The second best time is now"

Here's a simple timeline to show a possible order of progression. It is not intended to be instructional or rigid, just an example of where / how you could get started.

Start by using up what you've got.

⬇

Commit to buying no more new stuff unless absolutely necessary

⬇

Research alternatives of what can be used once you have run out.

⬇

Monitor what you put in the bin...find new uses for materials that are regularly binned.

⬇

Treat yourself to some new eco products as and when you genuinely need them.

⬇

By this time you will have been able to research what's available and no doubt have saved some pennies along the way.

Keep educating yourself on the climate crisis and find new ways of making a change.

A LOAD OF OLD RUBBISH?

Here are some tips and ideas of how you could save some items from the bin by repurposing them.

Tooth brushes can be used for scrubbing difficult to reach places, between tiles, plug holes, corners, the bottoms of cutlery drainers and many more places.

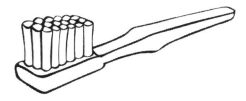

Collect onion, lemon and garlic net packaging and place one inside of the other. When you have a tennis ball sized collection, tie a knot in the top and use as a **scourer**.

Cut up old clothes, sheets, pillow cases and towels and store for use as **rags**. They can even be used as kitchen worktop cloths, cleansing wipes, removing nail polish, window cleaning and instead of paper kitchen towel for mopping up spillages. You could colour code, or use different patterns for different uses. Old sheets and pillowcases are great for window cleaning whereas more synthetic fabrics work well as **nail polish removers**.

Cut up the legs of old tights into rings which can be repurposed as **hairbands**.

A LOAD OF OLD RUBBISH?

Toilet rolls

Experiment with some different toilet rolls until you find an ethical/eco brand that suits you.

Think about where it is made - how far it has to travel and what it is wrapped in.

You could also look up the eco-credentials of the company. Do they invest in people, donate to charity, support regeneration programmes? Look out for greenwashing.

Don't assume that because the rolls appear to cost more money per pack or per roll that they are more expensive.
For example, the toilet rolls I use are 4 ply rather than the 2 ply ones I used to buy.

There are also significantly more sheets per roll meaning that they do actually work out cheaper even if it doesn't seem that way to start with.

Try to look beyond the gimmicks, and don't be afraid to try out a few different brands before settling on one. When you are happy with your choice, I recommend buying as many as you have the space to store in bulk - this will save you money and time. You won't have to restock for ages!

A LOAD OF OLD RUBBISH?

Once you have finished with the loo roll and have a cardboard tube left behind - don't bin it straight away... there are lots of things you can make or do with it first....

Christmas crackers - a homemade sweet treat, mini soap, bath bomb, a joke and a fabric crown, or homemade paper one made from newspaper, or decorated brown paper. Get the kids involved in making and decorating these in the lead up to Christmas. You can even buy bangers online for homemade crackers.

Bird feeder - pierce a hole through the tube thread some string through for hanging up with. Roll the tube in peanut butter and then seeds.
Insert a rod or stick through another two holes for the bird to stand on.

A gift box - wrap the outside with a pretty paper or decorate. Put the small item inside the tube and then flatten each end. Wrap with ribbon.

Seedling pots - Find a tray (old plastic fruit trays are good) and use an old spoon to add compost into each. Add your seeds and then water gently. When the seedlings are ready to be potted on, they can be added in their tub to the ground or pot - they will compost straight into the ground.

A LOAD OF OLD RUBBISH?

Banana skins

Did you know how good banana skins are for plants?

They are an excellent source of potassium and magnesium which will benefit both houseplants and garden plants. Tomatoes and roses particularly love them.

Banana tea for feeding plants. You can chop the banana into small pieces and soak in water. Use the water (banana tea) in a watering can to feed your plants and dig the chopped banana skin straight into the soil or compost.

If you are short for time or space, you can just chuck them into your compost as they are, but it is worth chopping up into smaller pieces if you can.

Before using them for compost, whole banana skins can also be rubbed on plant leaves to nourish and polish them - a great way to **dust and refresh house plants.**

On a sunny day, or in the bottom of a warm oven you can also dry out whole banana skins and then grind or blend the dried skins to **a powder which can be sprinkled into plant pots** to directly nourish the plant. I love doing this in the summer - it actually smells delicious when blended to a powder and my roses are clearly very happy!

A LOAD OF OLD RUBBISH?

Egg shells

Wash your egg shells after use and then collect them in a pot (I use an old large yogurt pot for this purpose).

When the pot is full you can crush the shells (I use a food blender to get a really fine dust). The crushed egg shells will add nutrients (including calcium) to soil and also make it difficult for slugs and snails to get to your plant if you sprinkle it around the base of the plants.

Some people keep the shells intact and then plant seedlings straight into the egg shell. They use the egg box to hold them upright. When ready to be planted out or potted up, the eggshell can go directly into the ground.

Brown paper bags and used kitchen towel

Can be torn into tiny pieces and added to a compost bin. Sometimes I keep my paper bags whole and stuff them full of veg peels and put into the compost bin as it is.

Foil

Rather than throwing little bits of foil here and there into the recycling. Save it up in a ball until you have a ball at least the size of a tennis ball so that the recycling processing machines can detect it more easily.

A LOAD OF OLD RUBBISH?

Tea bags / Tea leaves

Did you know that MANY tea bags are made from plastic and are therefore not compostable?

I was so shocked when I heard this!

Disappointed for the environment, my compost pile and also the fact that I drink so many cups of tea a day unknowingly. I've been drinking something that has steeped in a plastic casing in boiling water surely this cannot be good for my health.

I've since switched to loose tea leaves, and found a few brands which make it known that their tea bags are plastic free and compostable.

Plastic free tea bags and loose leaves can also be added to compost whereas those which are not plastic free will not break down properly.

Why not switch your tea bag brand, or even try out using tea leaves?

I haven't done the sums, but I think I'm spending less on the loose tea leaves as they don't seem to need replacing as often as the boxes of tea bags I used to buy.

A LOAD OF OLD RUBBISH?

Buy less packaging

If your goal is to buy and chuck out less packaging, here are a few things to think about and some suggestions of solutions too.

Fruit and veg packaging can really mount up...

Fruit and veg have their own natural packaging in the form of peel. We can scrub or peel them before eating them if we want to. There really is no need to wrap them in layers of plastic.

Why not commit to buying more loose veg and bringing your own bags. Collect up old bread bags and cereal packets, along with any other bags that might otherwise go straight in the bin and keep them in one of your reusable shopping bags in the car boot. That way you will never be caught short.

Alternatively seek out a farm shop or green grocer where there are more options of loose veg on offer. Maybe they will deliver to you to save you making an extra shopping trip out?

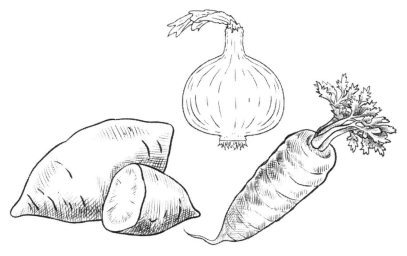

A LOAD OF OLD RUBBISH?

Or find a veg box scheme which works for you.
Think about what is important to you in a veg box scheme before you start your search...

Do you want organic only?
Do you need a flexible scheme?
Is local produce most important to you?
How much do you want to spend?
Do you need it to be delivered?

Once you know what your priorities are, it will be easier to make the choice between the many options out there.
I procrastinated for a long time before committing to a veg box scheme.

The commitment to a subscription like this, and knowing that there is another box arriving in a week means that I am also more eager to eat up all the fruit and veg to avoid waste before my next delivery. Consequently we have started planning meals around the veg we have to use up and we are all eating A LOT more fruit and veg and enjoying a wider range of seasonal veg as well.

Both are valuable added bonuses on top of the reduction of plastic going through our household.

A LOAD OF OLD RUBBISH?

No more clingfilm

There are so many alternatives to clingfilm ... and some of them are FREE! Once you've found an alternative you are happy with you will wonder why on earth you EVER spent money on the dratted stuff.

Save up **bread bags, cereal packets, crisp packets, cheese wrappers, frozen pea bags** whatever you can lay your hands on... all of these can be used to put your sandwiches in or to slip an opened packet into. Some are even zip lock or sealable bags - for free! Alternatively seal it with a bit of tape (paper kraft tape is far better than sellotape) if you need to. If you use the **paper tape, a felt tip pen** can be used to write a label on the tape so that you know what is inside.

Use **greaseproof paper** to wrap your sarnies in, or around a fresh loaf of bread, buns, cakes - whatever. You can easily write on the outside of the paper to say which sandwich filling you have used, or who the sandwiches belong to.

Buy some **silicone lids** - you can get sets of several different sizes- they will last for ages and can be stretched around half cut fruit such as melons, apples, oranges and lemons to keep the cut side fresh until you need it next.

NO TO PLASTIC

A LOAD OF OLD RUBBISH?

No more cling film
Use old jam jars for leftovers in the fridge - they are see through so you can see what's in there and you won't need any clingfilm.

When microwaving food in a bowl - add a plate to the top of the bowl instead of cling film to stop water bubbling over or explosions from happening.

Buy or make some waxed fabric wraps - the wax means that you can mould the fabric around whatever it is that you are wrapping. You could make your own with some cotton rags that you have cut up from an old duvet, pillow or shirt.

Make more use of plastic milk bottles
Old plastic milk bottles can be washed out then use a needle or pin to push small holes into the lid. The bottle makes an excellent gentle watering can for watering delicate seedlings and smaller house plants. The best thing is, you can have plenty of them dotted at strategic places around the house and garden for easy access regular waterings.

Another thing you can do with old bottles is to turn them upside down and pierce holes into the lid then insert the top of the bottle into a plant pot or flower bed near to your plants and use as a slow watering system - a great trick for when you are going away for a few days.

SMALL CHANGES
CAN MAKE A

BIG

DIFFERENCE
WHEN THEY FORM
NEW HABITS

Some small cost free changes we can all make right now

Walk
When time is not tight, ask yourself
"Do I really need to drive?
Can I walk or cycle instead?"

Turn off lights and appliances.
When you leave a room... switch off the light.
Unplug unused appliances overnight.
Stop charging phones and laptops overnight - most do not
require 8 hours to charge - an hour is often sufficient - why not
plug in first thing whilst you get ready for work or school in the
morning?

Never throw out old fabrics
What can they be used for instead?
Would someone else be able to make use of them?
Can they be repurposed into cleaning cloths?
Pretty fabrics can be used to wrap gifts - search up Furoshiki to
find out more and get some inspiration.

Eco changes do not have to cost the earth

Decant bulk buys
Decant things you have bought in bulk such as pasta, rice, cleaning products etc into glass jars or repurposed plastic tubs.

Eat less meat and fish
Explore alternative dishes - Shepherd's pie with lentils for example.

BYO cup
Get in the habit of bringing your own cup out with you. The more you do it, the more ingrained this habit will become. This can also be applied to picking up a cuppa from the work canteen - sometimes we forget these things when we cross the threshold of work.

Buy second hand
Explore buying second hand versions of things... Get into the habit of looking at what's available second hand before you look for new. Make buying new things a last resort.
I'm a sucker for preloved furniture, ornaments and jewellery. They have soul, a story and a patina you can't replicate with new. They are often far better quality, more unique and you can make small changes to make them your own.

Likewise with preloved clothes, you'll save £££, you will find things that suit you rather than the latest trend and you'll be giving a new life to something.
Teach your children to value preloved items in the same way. If we all do this, maybe we can slow down the demand for production of new items and slow down the output of all that waste that has to go somewhere... **One day there will be nowhere left for new waste but on our own doorstep.**

ECO GIVING

Cards and gifts

Have you ever thought about how much single use packaging and potential waste gifts and cards create?

What do you do with old cards, wrapping paper and gift bags? Don't throw any of it away - it can ALL be used again!

Re-use gift bags, and encourage others to do so with the bags that you give them.

Cards can be repurposed as gift tags, or made into a new card or more with some scissors and a glue stick.

Get creative with ribbons and pretty papers to create new and uniquely wrapped gifts.

You can also **re-use brown paper packaging**. Invest in a rubber stamp and ink pad and you can decorate your own paper.

Pretty ribbons can be cut off of clothing (the bits which are there to help hang clothing on to hangers) and saved.

Toilet rolls come in pretty handy in a shoe box to store different coloured ribbons and beads to accessorise gift wrap with.

Think how much money and resources you will save by making this small change. If you start building up a little box of goodies now, you will never get caught short... no more last minute dashes to shops, for hastily bought gift wrap and cards.

Not crafty?

Keep your eye on lovely gifts that you see advertised or mentioned on social media through the year. Buy to support **small traders locally** and save the things you buy in a box or cupboard. These will come in handy for gifts through the year and at Christmas.

SMALL CHANGE BIG DIFFERENCE

Make your own gifts...

I don't know about you, but I would far rather receive a thoughtful handmade gift than more "stuff" that is packaged from a shop. Here are some things you could think about gifting:

Bath bombs
Plants grown on as babies from your own plants
Hand picked wild flowers
Homemade chocolates
Homemade biscuits, jam, cakes or pastries
Home grown fruit and veg
Make a hamper of lovely homemade and home grown products
Pay for a day out, or experience and wrap up a note to explain the gift in some paper or a little fabric bag instead.

*Don't forget- **sellotape is plastic**, it contaminates boxes and wrapping paper from being recycled and it does not break down. Switch from sellotape to brown kraft tape or paper washi tape for friendlier alternatives

Use a hole punch to create **homemade confetti** from leaves. This is unique, pretty, free and sustainable!

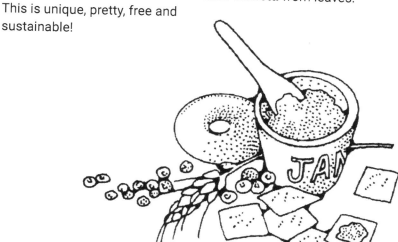

Cleaner cleaning

Where to start...

As with any change in products, you should really commit to using up what your already have, or alternatively passing it on for someone else to make use of. Whilst you are sorting out your existing products you can do a bit of research to find out what is on the market as eco friendly alternatives.

An easy first step would be to find a brand which has a good ethical profile in keeping with your own ideals. Or you might want to have a go at making some of your own products.

In this chapter I will outline the uses of some of the most basic of ingredients. Most of these come in cardboard packaging and are non-toxic to aquatic life, animals and humans. I really hate the idea of cleaning my home with chemicals which are ultimately not healthy for me or my family to breathe in and so I aim to use only the most basic of ingredients when cleaning my home.... And guess what... they are just as effective - I don't feel that I have compromised at all on functionality and the savings I've made are significant.

The only things that take a bit of getting used to are lack of colour and fragrance - however with a few essential oils the fragrance can be added back if you like.

Here are my favourite products

Bicarbonate of soda
Bio D washing up liquid
White vinegar
(buy in bulk 4 x 5 Litre bottles)
Soda crystals
Citric acid
Borax substitute
Soap nuts
Essential oils

CLEANER CLEANING

DIY cream cleaner recipe

Add a scoop of bicarbonate of soda or soda crystals into a small dish and then a squirt of washing up liquid.
Stir in a splash of water - enough to make into a spreadable paste.

This fabulous paste can be used anywhere that you would usually use a shop bought cream cleaner. It can be used on oven shelves and door, scuff marks on skirting boards and grubby areas around door frames and door handles. I've also used it on tiles, saucepans, kitchen cupboard door fronts and inside cupboards and drawers, and best of all the tops of kitchen cupboards and cooker hoods. It's great for dissolving grease and getting rid of scuffs and marks whilst brightening up grubby surfaces. Make sure you wipe it away with a fresh clean wet cloth to get rid of any residue. I like to apply it with an old toothbrush before wiping away with a clean cloth.

This recipe is as effective as any shop bought one.... In fact, I think you'll be surprised at how little scrubbing is needed.

Also it is ridiculously cheap - especially if you buy the bicarb in cardboard boxes of 500g rather than the tiny plastic tubs in the baking section of the supermarket.

Plus... it is plastic free. One less plastic bottle to add to the recycling bin!

Cleaner cleaning

All purpose de-greasing citrus cleaning spray recipe

- Keep a kilner jar or lidded jug in the cupboard under your sink.
- Half fill with white vinegar (not to be confused with white wine vinegar)
- Add lemon, orange and lime skins to the jug whenever you have them spare.
- Once the jug is full and the mixture has sat for a few weeks it can be decanted into an old spray bottle.
- Use a cleaning cloth or rag to line a funnel and pour the mixture into the bottle - this will help to filter out any stray bits of citrus fruit which could clog up the spray function.
- Half fill the cleaner bottle and then top up with water so that it is diluted 50/50

This spray can be used on tiles, splash backs, window sills, windows, bathroom surfaces, tables, windowsills, frames and kitchen worktops.

I use this product by spraying onto the surface and then wiping over it with a warm damp cloth or rag. It does not leave any residue and has a pleasant citrus smell. Don't worry about the odour of vinegar, this disappears very quickly and is not at all as strong as the malt vinegar you will be used to on chips.

A bonus of this homemade product is that if you are constantly collecting new lemon, lime or orange peels under the sink, and have a good supply of white vinegar in the house, you will never run out of it.

Again, this is ridiculously cheap especially if you buy the 5L bottles of white vinegar in bulk. I buy them in packs of 4 and only need order them once per year.

Cleaner cleaning

Bathroom cleaner

- Dissolve 1 tsp of borax in 500ml of hot water and leave to cool.
- Pour the cooled liquid into your empty spray bottle and then add 4 tbsp white vinegar or your own citrus infused vinegar spray
- Add a squirt of washing up liquid
- Add about 15 - 20 drops of an essential oil such as tea tree, eucalyptus, lavender, lemon or peppermint.

This spray can be used on all bathroom surfaces and wiped away with a damp cloth. It leaves my bathroom sparkling clean and smelling fresh.

Tiles and splashbacks

This tip makes use of a couple of my favourite eco cleaning ingredients. It's great for freshening up tiles, removing limescale build-up and greasy grime.

- Use white vinegar or your homemade citrus infused vinegar to firstly spray over the tile surfaces
- Then make up a cream cleaner paste of soda crystals, washing up liquid and a little water in a small bowl.
- Use an old toothbrush to apply the paste over the vinegar spray
- Then scrub the tile grout in between the tiles and in difficult to reach spots with an old toothbrush.
- Lastly use the shower head or a cloth soaked in hot water to rinse the tiles.
- Polish with a dry cloth to minimise water marks and give a lovely shine. I like to use my reusable bamboo kitchen roll for this job.

Remove limescale from taps and shower heads

- Add a scoop of citric acid or soda crystals to a small plastic bag... don't use a new bag, repurpose an old bread bag, cereal packet or carrier bag turned inside out, or add to a damp rag..
- Add a small amount of water and then use a hair band, elastic band or string to tie the bag/rag around the shower head or tap.
- Make sure the tap or showerhead is in full contact with the cleaning product. Leave (ideally overnight) and then rinse and wipe clean with a cloth after a few hours.

Clean your toilet the natural way
- Pour 100g citric acid or soda crystals into the loo
- Add hot water from a kettle and then leave to soak whilst you have a cup of tea.
- When you return to the loo, give it a good scrub with the loo brush or a wipe around if you prefer not to use a loo brush.
- Add a few drops of your favourite essential oil

Windows and mirrors

- Use white vinegar in a spray bottle to spritz over the glass window, shower screen or mirror.
- Immediately (don't leave it to dry) use a crunchy, crispy, dry old rag - old tea towels, sheets or pillow cases are perfect. I prefer natural fibres for this job as it needs to absorb the moisture. Rub vigorously with large circular movements. When the rag becomes damp switch to a new dry one. Clean both sides of the glass and don't stop until all smears are gone and the glass is completely dry.

  Don't worry about vinegar smell, it really doesn't last and will not be noticeable once you've finished the job.

Purify the air in your home

Get some houseplants to help purify the air in your home - the following are known to be especially good at this... Sansevieria (snake plant), Pothos (Devil's ivy), Peace lily, spider plant and rubber plant. I like to pit mine up to a larger pot once or twice a year as I love really large plants. This part is up to you!

Cleaner cleaning

Descale your kettle
- Add a small cup of white vinegar or citrus infused vinegar into the kettle or alternatively a small scoop of citric acid added to the kettle.
- Turn on the kettle and boil.
- Then pour away and rinse thoroughly before use for drinks.

Plug holes and drains
- Pour a generous amount of soda crystals into a kitchen sink or bathroom plughole, enough that it sits in the plug hole rather than going down.
- Leave to sit for 30 minutes - have a cup of tea!
- Boil the kettle and then pour down the plug hole

Mopping the kitchen or bathroom floor
- Hot water, a splash of citrus infused white vinegar and a tiny squirt of washing up liquid can be used together for a sparkling clean floor. Alternatively to get it really squeaky clean use a scoop of soda crystals in hot water - I only ever need to use the first option, however it does depend on how grimy floors get between cleans.

Dishwasher rinse aid
- Use white vinegar instead of rinse aid in the dishwasher.

Lovely laundry

There is more than one way to skin a cat (so they say) and there are **loads of eco tips and tricks for washing** as well as a wealth of new products to explore that will have significantly less impact on the environment, you and your family than current mainstream products do.

Open your mind, try out a few different products and methods before you decide which ones work for you.

I tried out a lot of different eco laundry options before I found the ones that work for me.
Everyone is different, so when you decide that you are ready to make some changes to your laundry habits, be open minded and remember, this is a journey, be prepared to try a few different ideas before you find one that works for you.

One thing that people find difficult when switching is the scent. Many people enjoy a strong fresh aroma with clean washing and associate this with cleanliness. You may have to wean yourself off this and gradually try products with less scent before you are happy. **My favourite scent for my washing now is the sunshine on the line smell - can't beat it!**
I also love the smell of soap nuts laundry which just smells "clean" to me.
Occasionally I use peppermint essential oil on my soapnuts bag - this is a lovely fresh scent and does seem to linger beyond the wash.

Before you try anything new.... Detox your machine

No need to buy a special pack to do this
(an unnecessary cost and packaging)... simply make use of
these every day basic cleaning products and run the longest
hottest cycle on your machine before the next use.

- Give the machine including the dispenser drawer and
seal a spray and wipe with some white vinegar, or citrus
infused white vinegar spray (homemade). Use a
toothbrush to get into the fiddly bits.
- You can usually remove the dispenser drawer to give it a
soak and a scrub if it's bad.
- Once the dispenser drawer is clean and back in place,
pour a cup of white vinegar into the softener
compartment.
- Add a cup full of soda crystals or citric acid to the drum.
- Run your machine on the hottest, longest cycle.

I promise, you will notice a difference. This should be done once
a month ideally to keep the limescale at bay and to get rid of
bacteria and mould buildup which can cause pongs and an
unfresh smell in your washing.

LAUNDRY ALTERNATIVES

Eco Egg

This is a plastic egg shaped casing which is filled with mineral pellets. It can be split in half to refill when needed. There are three scent options which come in three different **pretty pastel colours.**

The first egg you buy will cost around £10 and will last for 70 washes. After that, you can keep using the egg casing and simply buy refills which work out at around a fiver for 50 washes.

The mineral pellets work together in the water to **effectively draw dirt** from your clothes and softens them by changing the pH, thus leaving your laundry **clean and fresh without using harmful chemical** laden detergents.

The mineral pellets in the Eco Egg are **non-biological** and do not contain any petrochemicals, enzymes, bleaches, phosphates, parabens, SLS/SLES, palm oil or microplastics. This makes them **gentle** - perfect for those with sensitive skin and for aquatic life and the environment.

As the eco egg doesn't just suddenly stop working after the first 50 washes, you will never run out or get caught short. You'll be able to continue to use your egg whilst you wait for a refill pack to be delivered.

Possible drawbacks - some people report that they can't smell the scent enough. If this is the case try adding some drops of essential oil to the softener dispenser draw.

It is also advised not to wash with the eco egg over 50°C. So this is when I'd swap out my eco egg for another product instead on the rare occasions that I want to do a 60°C wash.

Laundry alternatives

Soap nuts

I was so excited to discover these. They are the most natural, raw form of washing product that you can find.

The Indian Soapberry or Soapnut is an ugly looking shriveled brown squishy shell. It does not smell or look anything special at all. But in rural India it is highly prized; the wood is used in construction and the fruit as a source of revenue.

Ecologically it is a sustainable, entirely renewable resource; the fruit is harvested and sun-dried, the seeds removed and planted to ensure crops for future generations.

The organically-grown berries contain a high proportion of  natural saponin or mild soap which is gentle on sensitive skin. They can be used for washing laundry simply by Placing 4-6 of them in a small cloth bag and placing in the drum of your washing machine.

Alternatively, you can make a multitude of cleaning products yourself from the soapnuts.

Some tips for using Soap nuts include:

Adding some drops of your favourite essential oil to the bag and/or soap dispenser/softener drawer will add a scent to your washing if this is what you like. Soapnuts do not have a smell as such. I find that the washing just comes out smelling "clean".

The used soap nut shells will last 4 - 5 washes and will then need to be replaced. When you have finished with the soapnuts, simply add them to your compost and they will keep the slugs and snails at bay!

The soap nuts come in a large cloth bag - in batches of 1KG (480 washes) for just over a tenner and 500g (240 washes) for just under a tenner. Bargain!

A mini cloth bag is also supplied with them which can be reused many, many times. So no harmful packaging sitting around in landfill for hundreds of years. These are easy, clean and fuss free to use, and my absolute favourite so far!

LAUNDRY ALTERNATIVES

Bio-D laundry liquid

I absolutely love this brand and use many of their products. I usually buy their 5L bottles and refill smaller bottles as they do still come in plastic bottles - though they are made from recycled plastic and are recyclable).

Plastic bottles aside, these products are so ethically sound in so many ways, so effective and smell absolutely wonderful.

A bit about the brand - Made in Hull, UK and have complete traceability on all the ingredients they use so that we can be confident that they are ethically and sustainably sourced - all products are vegan, cruelty free, scientifically tested against allergies, BRC global standards certificated and listed as an Ethical consumer best buy.

You won't find any of the following list of nasties in any of the other Bio D products: Chemical plasticisers, formaldehyde, glycerin or glycerine, sodium tallowate, synthetic dyes, synthetic perfumestitanium dioxide, benzisothiazolinone, phthalates, phosphates, E.D.T.A, genetically engineered enzymes, optical brighteners, urea, lanolin, MI, MCI, tallow, triclosan, chlorine bleaches, petroleum-derived additives.

The laundry liquid is as effective as any other laundry liquid I've used, but has a gentler scent and is colourless. The fragrances available are lavender, Juniper or fragrance free. This is a good first step option to use whilst you try out other options. It comes in standard sized bottles as well as the 5L ones.

Bio D also does a super dooper washing up liquid.
This comes in Various scents - my favourite is the pink grapefruit. It also comes fragrance free.
It washes as well as any other washing liquid I've used, if not better and has a lovely scent and is gentle on the hands. I would not swap back to any other brand of washing up liquid now.

Laundry - General Advice

Machine and product maintenance
In between washes, leave your washing machine drawer open and leave products such as the eco egg or soap nuts pouch on top of the machine to air out and dry.
This prevents musty smells and dampness.

De-odourising
Make a paste of bicarb of soda and a tiny amount of water to rub onto stinky armpits to diffuse pongy patches of laundry. Spread it on the offending area for a few minutes (or longer if you like) before washing as normal in the machine.

Add a scoop of bicarb to the washing drum before washing to neutralise general odours in the load

Stain removal
Add a scoop of soda crystals to the soap dispenser drawer of drum for extra stain busting power with a heavily soiled load.

or

Use the Dri-pak product called Oxi-boost either as a paste on the stain 20 minutes before washing, in a soak for 1 hour before washing or in your machine with the usual detergent for general lightening and brightening. Oxi-boost comes in a cardboard box which can be easily recycled.

or

Living naturally have a stain remover bar which contains no artificial dyes or perfumes, just the fresh, clean scent of natural eucalyptus as well as the deodorizing power of litsea and it will not discolour clothes or fabrics. No plastic packaging - just a paper sleeve.

Laundry - General advice

To soften hard water
Add a couple of tablespoons of Oxi-Boost, soda crystals or Borax substitute to your washing machine - by softening the water, you will require less washing powder or liquid and therefore save money!

Instead of softener
White vinegar can be added to the softener compartment of the dispenser drawer in your machine. This will also help to keep limescale build up at bay and prevent static in your clothes. Use the same amount as what you would usually use of softener. Don't worry - the vinegar smell will have disappeared by the time you remove your clothes from the wash.

Keep your whites white
Add some Oxi - Boost or Borax substitute to the detergent drawer. A couple of tablespoons should be enough, but if you live in a hard water area, you may need to use more.

Keep pongs at bay

Bicarbonate of soda is fantastic at eliminating nasty whiffs. You can make your very own shaker dispenser with an old spice jar or a flour or icing sugar dredger - you can then shake and vac or add a sprinkle to the bottoms of bins easily! You could even add a few drops of your favourite essential oil to the pot for extra fragrance. This can be sprinkled on carpets, sofas, cushions, animal beds etc. Hoover up when it has had a few hours to work it's magic.

Once a month or so, sprinkle some bicarbonate of soda on mattresses and leave whilst you wash the bedding. Vacuum it up before making the bed up again. This will neutralise odours and remove dust mites.

Sprinkle some bicarbonate of soda into old cleaned jam jars that you are saving as well as tupperware. This will mean you can keep lids on so they don't get lost and that nasty stale smell won't be a problem. Tip out the bicarb of soda before use and give the jar or tub a quick rinse or wipe.

An Unconventional cleaning aid.

Use a 2 pence piece to rub against baking trays and oven shelves with homemade bicarb cream cleaner paste to remove burnt on bits from the bottom of a baking tray or pan.

Lovely lemons

Add a lemon skin to the microwave and heat for 30 seconds - 1 minute then wipe clean - easy peasy, no more nast whiffs and a squeaky clean microwave.

Wipe over stainless steel surfaces such as sink and drainer with a used lemon skin - it will degrease, clean and leave a super sparkle and shine.

Wipe a used chopping board with a used lemon to remove odours and grease.

HOUSEHOLD - GENERAL ADVICE

Water - the planet's most precious resource

Don't throw water down the drain. Keep a watering can in the kitchen to collect the dregs of water from glasses and jugs. Use it to water the plants, or grass.

Once you are using less toxic cleaning products you can throw out the dishwater, bucket water, bath water on the lawn or collect in a watering can. This will mean that you use less water to keep your plants happy and healthy.

Cooled pasta or rice water from cooking are nutritious for plants. Add them to your watering can and dilute with plain water.

Water the plants

Old plastic milk bottles can be washed out. Use a needle or pin to push small holes into the lid. The bottle makes an excellent gentle watering can for watering delicate seedlings and smaller house plants. The best thing is, you can have plenty of them dotted at strategic places around the house and garden for easy access regular waterings.

No more ironing

Hang your washing on the line as soon as the weather is relatively dry., Give everything a vigorous shake to remove creases and hang clothes directly onto hangers on a portable clothes rail. They can then be brought in easily at the first sign of rain, a neighbour having a fire or overnight. Clothes can then be hung up straight away to eliminate the need for ironing (more electricity) or folding (more time).

Natural stain remover

Did you know that sunlight helps to lighten whites and remove stains. And not forgetting that fresh air and sunshine smell - in my book, nothing can beat that!

Personal Care

The more I look into personal care, the more I've realised that simple is best. A short list of ingredients - hopefully ones I recognise, simple or no packaging and less products are best. I've found that by using the simpler products they can often do a number of different jobs and therefore I need one product in place of where I use to have several.

Shower power
Stop buying plastic cloths, scrubbies, mitts and sponges. Instead use a natural sponge, loofah or cotton flannel. You can also get little bags for collecting soap bits in which can be used as scrubbies too.

A Soaper Easy swap
This was honestly the easiest and most rewarding swap I ever did. **Swap shower gel for soap.**
Choose a gentle, kind soap which is not wrapped in plastic and invest in a simple soap dish or soap tin to keep your soap from getting too soggy.

I love The Friendly Soap range the best, but there are many others that are out there too. You may need to try a few before you find your favourite.

Make up / break up
Make or buy reusable cloth make-up wipes for your face. Have a little pot or net bag for used ones to go in near to where you cleanse your face. If you use a drawstring bag they can be put straight in the wash like that. This is a great use for old flannels, towels, dressing gowns which you can chop up into smaller pieces and store in a pretty box or tub.

Make your own bath bombs

These can make lovely (plastic free) gifts, as well as being a fun activity to do with children.

What a great end of term gift idea for their teacher!.

Recipe:

100g bicarbonate of soda

50g citric acid

25g cornflour

2bsp oil

10 drops essential oil

A few drops of food colouring (optional)

Lavender or rose petals, or an opened herbal tea bag

A few drops of water

- Mix together the dry ingredients in bowl
- Add the wet ingredients to a small bowl and mix
- Slowly add the wet ingredients to the dry whilst stirring
- You may not need all of the water - be sparing with it.
- Pack the mixture into moulds such as old yogurt pots, ice cube trays .
- Store in the fridge overnight.

Bake your own snacks

Start baking your own food products from scratch: e.g. bread, biscuits, cakes, curries, popcorn, crisps, chips. Think about how much packaging you will be able to avoid. The plus side of this is that you will also know exactly the ingredients used and you can play around and tweak recipes until they suit you and your family best.

Bread making is a lengthy process, but in reality, the hard work put in by you is just 5 mins of kneading, 1 minute of shaping and 1 minute of weighing ingredients. The rest of the time, the bread will be either proving or baking. No more plastic bread bags, and you'll benefit from the aroma of lovely freshly baked bread.

Bake a couple of loaves at a time to last the week. Bread can be sliced and frozen too for ease of use. Frozen bread slices can be popped straight into the toaster for toast in the morning.

Sanitary wear

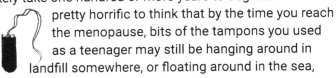

Many tampons and sanitary pads contain plastic. They will likely take one hundred or more years to degrade. It's pretty horrific to think that by the time you reach the menopause, bits of the tampons you used as a teenager may still be hanging around in landfill somewhere, or floating around in the sea, not to mention the wrappers?

There are a number of options that you could try to reduce this ridiculous amount of waste (and money) that results from disposable sanitary wear.
I have outlined a few below:

Silicone menstrual cups - These are inserted into your vagina and can be worn for periods of up to 12 hours at a time - this is fantastic as you won't need to change through the day until you are at home. It then needs to be washed, dried and reused. Simple. Many people absolutely swear by them. They come in varying sizes - there is even an extra small size for teenagers.

Period underwear - Whilst you might imagine period pants to be big and dowdy, this just isn't the case, there are loads of lovely feminine designs available which are comfy, discreet and effective. They can be worn all day and then soaked in a small bin in the bathroom before being washed. There are loads of designs and companies offering these. I recommend researching a few, looking for reviews and personal recommendations before investing. You would probably need a set of 5 - 7 pants to see you through your period, so there would be an initial outlay which is perhaps initially more of an outlay than the other options available, but if you like the idea of no extra faff, just a daily change of knickers then this could be the option for you and in the long term, this would work out financially viable.

PERSONAL CARE

Washable cloth pads - There are so many different washable cotton or bamboo pads - some of them organic. Different lengths, shapes., sizes, colours and patterns, attachments, fastenings. In fact some people have made this their entire business and can help you to find the exact right product for you based upon your own set of preferences, flow and need.

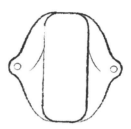

Eco friendly disposable pads - If you are not quite ready to explore the other options yet, there is the option of organic cotton or bamboo disposable sanitary pads or tampons. These would contain none of the chemicals of their plastic counterparts and their packaging is recyclable. The pads/ tampons are plastic free and biodegradable.

Again, this is a personal matter, and will vary very much from individual to individual so it is best to try a few and decide for yourself which works best for YOU!

FOR FUN!

Make your own playdough
400g Bicarbonate of Soda
100g corn flour
250ml water
1 tablespoon vegetable oil
food colourings of your choice

- Add all of the ingredients to a saucepan and mix well
  Slowly heat on a low temperature whilst stirring
- Do this until the mixture starts to thicken - a bit like
  mashed potato texture.
- Empty out onto a chopping board and cover with a damp
  tea towel until it is cool.
- Divide into smaller balls and add a different colour food
  colouring to weach ball by kneading it into the mixture.
- Dust the worktop with a little cornflour before playing.
- The dough will keep for a few days in a sealed tub, or
  creations can be left out to air dry and harden.

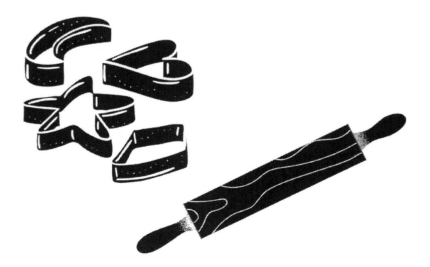

Recycling address book

Start an address book of places that items can be sent to be reused / repurposed. I have included a few here for you, however there will also be places more local to you that collect items such as batteries, print cartridges etc.

Old bras

Recycling Scheme
Against Breast Cancer
Leathem House
13 Napier Court
Barton Lane,
Abingdon, OXON, OX14 3YT

£1 per kilo of bras received is used to fund research into breast cancer. The useable bras are then donated to developing countries such as Togo, Ghana and Kenya, where bras remain too expensive to produce locally.

Usable cosmetics and toiletries

Give and Makeup
PO BOX 855
LONDON
W4 4AW

Old phones

Recycling your mobile with WaterAid is an easy and cost free way to help WaterAid transform the lives of some of the world's poorest people.
https://www.fonebank.com/wateraid

Miscellaneous

Send unwanted items including electrical items, clothing, jewellery and old video games by freepost with British Heart Foundation.
Get your freepost label here:
https://www.bhf.org.uk/shop/donating-goods/post-your-donations#what

Recycling address book

This website has a wealth of helpful information on the best way to recycle or dispose of most items responsibly.
https://www.recyclenow.com/what-to-do-with/

Some examples taken from the recycle now website are below:
Old inhalers should be returned to a local pharmacy for safe disposal. Did you know that landfill disposal of inhalers is harmful to the environment both in material waste and in greenhouse gas emissions as the residual gas from canisters is released to the atmosphere.

Medicine blister packets can also be collected and then dropped off at local pharmacies.

Most supermarkets have a collection point for **plastic bags and film** - why not set up a box or carrier bag for saving these up rather than chucking them in the bin.

You can sell your **broken or working old mobile phones** to companies online such as this one:
https://www.sellmymobile.com/
This website has really good advice on how to make sure your **data is wiped from your phone** before selling/ donating and also how to donate your old phone to charity.
http://www.reducereuserecycle.co.uk/

A friendly community.
For more hints, tips, shared problems and solutions.
Join my online group called
"**Going Eco together**"
https://www.facebook.com
/groups/777604852989751

Printed in Great Britain
by Amazon